P9-CKA-539

the spiralizer COOKBOOK

WILLIAMS-SONOMA
test kitchen

Photographs Maren Caruso

weldon**owen**

Contents

Welcome to Spiralizing 7

Spiralizer Blades 8

Spiralizing Primer 10

Tips and Tricks 13

Recipes 17

Index 52

Welcome to Spiralizing

The Spiralizer is a versatile kitchen tool that will change the way you cook. In the test kitchen, we use this innovative spiral slicer to create noodles, shoestrings, and thin shreds or slices from a wide variety of fruits and vegetables. We find that the Spiralizer is the perfect kitchen companion when we're developing recipes. It creates vegetable noodles in seconds, which are a great addition to a healthy lifestyle. Using the Spiralizer, you can also cut onions into rings, potatoes into chips, or sweet potatoes into curly fries in a fraction of the time it takes to cut them with a knife or other kitchen tool. Spiral-sliced vegetables can add novelty and nutrients to comfort food favorites—think macaroni and cheese made with spiralized butternut squash instead of pasta, or spiralized apples baked into a sweet, golden brown cake. The Spiralizer can also create a beautiful, colorful presentation without any extra effort or fancy garnishes. In short, it is the perfect tool for the creative home cook.

On the pages that follow, you'll discover a primer on how to use the Spiralizer to prepare a wide variety of different ingredients—from apples to onions to zucchini. Following are more than 20 recipes for using your Spiralizer in meals any time of the day. Try the Poached Eggs in Potato Nests (page 42) for a weekend brunch; the colorful and superfood-rich Beet, Fennel, and Carrot Salad (page 36) for a quick and nutritious workday lunch; or even Zucchini Spaghetti with Turkey Meatballs (page 18) for a new spin on a favorite family supper. Many of the recipes are healthy, and a few are indulgent, but all of them are designed to make the most of this innovative kitchen tool.

Spiralizer Blades

The Spiralizer comes with three blades, and each blade creates a unique shape.

What can be spiralized?

There is a wide range of fruits and vegetables that can be spiralized. For best results, the item should have a solid core.

- apples
- beets
- broccoli stalks
- butternut squash
- cabbage
- carrots
- cucumbers
- daikon
- fennel
- jicama
- kohlrabi
- onions
- pears
- potatoes
- radishes
- shallots
- sweet potatoes
- zucchini
- and more!

A The Straight Blade

This versatile blade creates a wide ribbon shape, similar to pappardelle pasta. This blade is also used to shred cabbage, slice onions and shallots, and shave potatoes into paper-thin slices for gratins or chips. It is also used to slice apples and pears for baking or fruit chips.

B The Chipper Blade

This blade produces a thick, round, noodle-like shape. It is used to create thick vegetable strands for baked dishes.

C The Shredder Blade

This blade makes thin, round noodles, akin to spaghetti. It works with a wide array of vegetables, which can be quickly sautéed for a pastalike dish, or left uncooked for a refreshing raw salad. These thin spirals can also be baked into pancakes or cakes.

Some Spiralizer models include a thinner version of the Shredder Blade, which forms strands similar to angel hair pasta. If you have this blade, experiment with using it for vegetable salads or ultrathin vegetable fries.

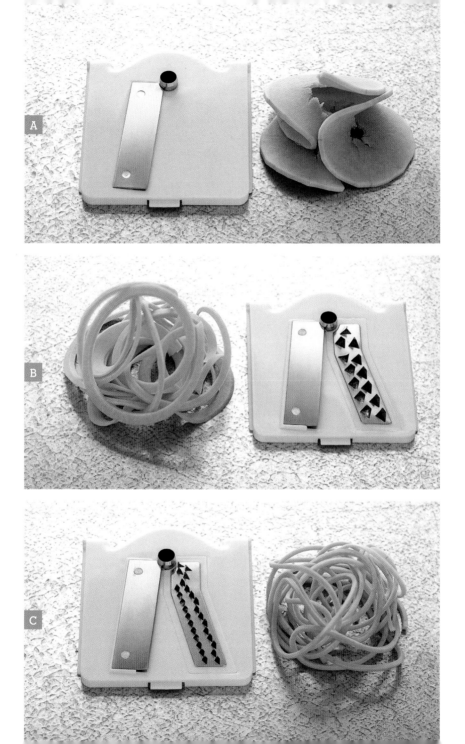

Spiralizing Primer

Working with the Spiralizer is a simple 6-step process. Consult the manufacturers' instructions to assemble the machine, then follow the steps below.

1 Place the Spiralizer on a nonporous work surface, like a counter top or marble board. Push firmly on the suction cups to secure the machine to the surface.

2 Place your desired blade into the top slot. The extra blades are stored in the plastic drawers on one side of the machine.

3 Prep your vegetables or fruit. Peel them, if necessary, then cut off both ends to create 2 straight, flat surfaces.

4 Align the vegetable (or fruit) such that the small cylindrical protrusion near the blade is positioned in the center. Once aligned, push the vegetable in firmly.

5 Holding the vegetable (or fruit) in one hand, use your other hand to slide the handle toward the vegetable. Push the teeth of the handle into the end of the vegetable until it holds securely.

6 Crank the handle, applying even pressure toward the blade. The spiralized vegetable or fruit will emerge from the other side of the machine; if desired, place a bowl on the other side of the Spiralizer to collect the food as it falls from the blade.

top slot for blade

blade

handle

suction cups

Spiralizing Tips & Tricks

Cooking with spiralized vegetables is easy, but keeping a few tips and tricks in mind will ensure best results in your finished dishes.

TIP 1 **Choose the right vegetable**

Use vegetables that are at least 2 inches in diameter. Thicker vegetables will be easier to attach to the machine and will cut more evenly.

TIP 2 **Center the food on the machine**

Be sure to carefully center the vegetable or fruit on the slicer. This will help create uniform cuts.

TIP 3 **Save time when slicing**

When slicing vegetables, such as apples, onions, pears, and potatoes, we use the Straight Blade, to save prep time. Using a chef's knife, cut a lengthwise slit down the side of the item, stopping just short of the center. Spiralize as usual to create slices.

TIP 4 **Cut or break your noodles**

Long, curly, spiralized vegetables look pretty on the plate, but they can be difficult to eat. To make vegetable noodles more manageable, use your hands or a pair of kitchen scissors to break or cut the noodles every few turns. You can also chop ingredients with a knife after spiralizing.

TIP 5 **Reduce moisture**

Vegetables and fruits contain high amounts of water. Follow the recipe cues for moderating the moisture to ensure a good result.

TIP 6 **Don't overcook**

Vegetable noodles cook quickly. Follow the cues in the recipes and avoid overcooking, which could cause them to become mushy.

TIP 7 **Working with cabbage**

When prepping cabbage, you only need to trim the top of the head. The core makes a great place to anchor the vegetable on the machine. If your cabbage is very tight and compact, try cutting 4 small slits around the circumference of the head (rather than the usual 1), creating an X shape towards the center. This can help create smaller shred lengths.

TIP 8 **Working with carrots**

For best yield, look for large "horse" carrots that don't taper too much. If you can't find wide carrots, readjust the position of the carrot on the Spiralizer frequently to help maintain consistency in the end result.

TIP 9 **Making curly fries**

Making classic curly fries is a snap with the Spiralizer. Use your preferred spiral blade to create curls of russet or Yukon gold potatoes. Fry them in 350°F oil until golden brown, then drain and season with salt. Consider other root vegetables for fries, too, such as sweet potatoes, rutabagas, and turnips. You may need to adjust the temperature of your oil and your frying time, depending on the sugar content of the vegetable.

TIP 10 **Working with fruit**

We found that the Spiralizer is a great way to slice fruit, as it doesn't require the cumbersome task of coring first. If any core remains after spiralizing, use a small cookie cutter to cut it away. Be sure to use firm pears when you are baking them after spiralizing. Ripe pears give off too much liquid, contributing to a soggy result.

14

Garlicky Beef & Broccoli

WITH BROCCOLI NOODLES

This version of a popular Chinese takeout dish gets a healthy update by adding extra broccoli and eliminating the heavy sauce. Freezing the steak for 30 minutes prior to slicing allows you to slice it easily.

In a large bowl, whisk together the cornstarch, sugar, salt, and 2 tablespoons water. Add the steak, toss to coat, and let stand for 30 minutes.

Remove the broccoli tops from the stems. Cut the tops into 1-inch florets. Trim the bottom 2 inches from the stalks, then peel the tough outer layer. Spiralize the stalks using the Shredder Blade and set aside.

Cook the noodles according to the instructions on the package. Drain and rinse with cold water; set aside.

In a large nonstick frying pan over medium-high heat, warm 1 tablespoon of the oil. Add the minced garlic and sauté for 30 seconds. Add the broccoli stalks and sauté until tender-crisp, about 2 minutes. Add the noodles and toss until heated through. Set aside and keep warm.

In a large nonstick frying pan over medium-high heat, warm 2 tablespoons of the oil. Add the garlic slices and pepper flakes. Stir-fry until crisp, about 1 minute. Remove the garlic with a slotted spoon; drain on paper towels.

Re-warm the oil. Add the broccoli florets and stir-fry until tender-crisp, 1–2 minutes; transfer to a plate. Wipe out the pan, add 2 tablespoons of the oil, and re-warm. Add half of the beef and stir-fry until medium-rare, about 2 minutes. Transfer to the plate with the broccoli and repeat to cook the remaining meat. Add the wine and tamari to the pan and stir for 30 seconds, scraping up any browned bits. Add the broccoli and meat back to the pan and toss to coat. Sprinkle with the crisp garlic slices.

Divide the rice and broccoli noodles among 4 plates. Top with the beef and broccoli and serve.

SERVES 4

Ingredients

1 tablespoon cornstarch

½ teaspoon sugar

¼ teaspoon kosher salt

1 lb flank or skirt steak, partially frozen, cut across the grain into 2-by-⅓-inch slices

2 heads broccoli (about 2 lb total weight), stems intact

8 oz thick brown rice noodles

5 tablespoons canola oil

1 clove garlic, minced, plus 3 cloves garlic, thinly sliced

¼ teaspoon red pepper flakes

3 tablespoons dry white wine

2 tablespoons tamari

TIP
Broccoli stalks are delicious when spiralized. Be sure to cut off 2 inches of the tough ends and peel the stems well before using.

Zucchini Spaghetti

WITH TURKEY MEATBALLS

This old-fashioned family favorite gets a healthy makeover with the use of ground turkey instead of beef and spiralized zucchini instead of pasta for a low-carb dinner that everyone will love.

½ cup olive oil

½ yellow onion, spiralized using the Straight Blade, then roughly chopped

Kosher salt and freshly ground pepper

1 lb ground turkey

1½ cups dried bread crumbs

1 egg, whisked

2 teaspoons chopped fresh sage

2 cans (28 oz/875 g each) whole plum tomatoes, preferably San Marzano, with juices

2 cloves garlic, minced

2 teaspoons soy sauce

1 teaspoon dried oregano

4 medium-sized zucchini

Grated Parmesan cheese for serving

In a large sauté pan over medium-high heat, warm 1 tablespoon of the oil. Add the onion and a few pinches of salt and sauté until soft, about 5 minutes. Transfer to a large bowl and let cool. Add the ground turkey, bread crumbs, egg, sage, 1 teaspoon salt, and ½ teaspoon pepper to the bowl and use your hands to mix the ingredients gently but thoroughly. Form the mixture into 12 equal-sized meatballs and place on a plate.

In the same sauté pan, warm 2 tablespoons of the oil over medium-high heat. Add the meatballs and cook until browned, about 1 minute per side. Transfer to a plate.

Put the tomatoes and their juices in a food processor. While pulsing, slowly add ¼ cup of the oil through the feed tube until the tomatoes are puréed but still a bit chunky. Stir in the garlic, soy sauce, and oregano and season to taste with salt and pepper. Pour the tomato sauce into the sauté pan, place over medium heat, and bring to a simmer. Add the meatballs, cover, and reduce the heat to low. Cook, stirring once or twice, until the meatballs are cooked through, about 30 minutes.

While the meatballs are cooking, spiralize the zucchini using the Shredder Blade. Toss with a pinch of salt and place in a colander; let the liquid drain from the zucchini.

When the meatballs are ready, in a large sauté pan over medium high heat, warm the remaining 1 tablespoon oil. When oil is hot, add the zucchini and sauté just until the zucchini is warm, about 30 seconds; do not overcook.

Divide the zucchini spaghetti, meatballs, and sauce among individual pasta bowls. Sprinkle with cheese and serve.

SERVES 4–6

Moroccan-Spiced Roasted Chicken

WITH CARROT SALAD

This dish is perfect for a busy night. The Spiralizer makes quick work of slicing the onions, which become a flavorful bed for spice-rubbed chicken. As the bird roasts, make the carrot salad to serve alongside.

Preheat the oven to 425°F.

In a small bowl, combine the turmeric, 2 teaspoons salt, 1 teaspoon of the cumin, the garlic powder, coriander, thyme, cinnamon, and pepper. Sprinkle the spice mixture all over the chicken.

Cut a slit in one side of each onion, stopping near the center. Spiralize the onions using the Straight Blade. Transfer the onions to a bowl and toss with 2 tablespoons of the oil.

Spread the onions in a roasting pan and add ¼ cup water. Place a roasting rack over the onions and arrange the chicken, breast-side up, on the rack. Tuck the wings under the bird. Roast the chicken until the skin is browned and a thermometer inserted into the thickest part of the thigh, away from the bone, registers 165°F, 50–60 minutes. Transfer the chicken to a cutting board to rest. Stir the onions and transfer them to a serving platter; keep warm.

In a small bowl, whisk together the lemon juice, honey, 1 teaspoon salt, remaining ½ teaspoon cumin, and remaining 2 tablespoons olive oil. Set aside.

Spiralize the carrots using the Shredder Blade, stopping to break or cut the strands every 3–4 rotations. Transfer to a large bowl. Add the raisins, chopped cilantro, and lemon-honey mixture to taste, and toss well to coat.

Carve the chicken into 10 serving pieces and arrange on top of the onions on the platter. Garnish with cilantro leaves and serve with the carrot salad on the side.

1 tablespoon ground turmeric

Kosher salt

1½ teaspoons ground cumin

½ teaspoon garlic powder

½ teaspoon ground coriander

½ teaspoon dried thyme

½ teaspoon ground cinnamon

¼ teaspoon freshly ground pepper

1 whole chicken, about 4 lb

2 yellow onions, peeled and ends trimmed

4 tablespoons olive oil

3 tablespoons fresh lemon juice

1 tablespoon honey

1½ lb thick carrots, peeled and trimmed

3 tablespoons raisins

¼ cup chopped fresh cilantro or mint, plus cilantro leaves for garnish

SERVES 4–6

Greek-Style Chicken Pitas

WITH CUCUMBER SALAD & HERBED YOGURT SAUCE

Using the Spiralizer's straight blade allows you to create a bright salad for a grilled chicken pita in a fraction of the time it takes to use a knife. For extra flavor, you can marinate the chicken for up to 12 hours.

FOR THE HERBED YOGURT

1 cup Greek yogurt

1 clove garlic, minced

1½ tablespoons fresh lemon juice

4 tablespoons chopped fresh mint

Kosher salt

1 small red onion, peeled and ends trimmed

⅓ cup red wine vinegar

1 lemon

3 tablespoons olive oil

3 cloves garlic, minced

1½ tablespoons chopped fresh oregano

1½ tablespoons chopped fresh basil

1 lb boneless skinless chicken breasts, pounded to ½-inch thickness

Kosher salt and freshly ground pepper

1 English cucumber, ends trimmed

1 cup cherry tomatoes, halved (about 5½ oz)

2 oz feta cheese, crumbled

4 rounds pita bread, split

To make the herbed yogurt, combine all the ingredients in a small bowl and stir until well combined. Season to taste with salt. Cover and refrigerate until ready to use.

Cut a slit in one side of the onion, stopping near the center. Spiralize the onion using the Straight Blade and transfer to a bowl. Add the vinegar and let stand at room temperature, stirring occasionally, for 2 hours.

Finely grate the zest from the lemon then squeeze the juice. In a bowl, combine the lemon zest and juice, olive oil, garlic, oregano, and basil. Add the chicken and toss well to combine. Cover and refrigerate for 2 hours.

Heat a stove-top grill pan over medium-high heat. Remove the chicken from the marinade and season lightly with salt and pepper. Cook the chicken until it has nice grill marks and is cooked through, 3–4 minutes per side. Transfer to a cutting board to rest.

While chicken rests, cut a slit in one side of the cucumber, stopping before the seeded core. Spiralize the cucumber using the Straight Blade and transfer to a large bowl. Drain the vinegar from the onion, reserving the vinegar, and add the onion to the bowl with the cucumber. Add the tomatoes and feta cheese. Toss until well mixed, adding the reserved vinegar and salt to taste.

Slice the chicken, then divide it among the split pitas. Divide the cucumber salad among the sandwiches, drizzle each with the herbed yogurt, and serve.

SERVES 4

Shrimp Pad Thai

WITH DAIKON NOODLES

Spiralized daikon adds extra nutrients to this fresh take on pad Thai. Pad Thai sauce is surprisingly easy to make, but if you are in a hurry, use quality prepared sauce found where Asian ingredients are sold.

To make the sauce, in a small saucepan, combine the garlic, chile, palm sugar, tamarind paste, and fish sauce. Warm over medium heat, stirring occasionally, until the sugar has dissolved, 5–10 minutes if using palm sugar and 2–3 minutes if using brown sugar. Remove from the heat and stir in the lime juice.

Spiralize the daikon using the Shredder Blade, stopping to break or cut the strands every 3–4 rotations. Place the daikon in a large bowl and set aside. Next, spiralize the carrots, stopping to break or cut the strands every 3–4 rotations. Put the carrots in a separate bowl.

In a large nonstick sauté pan over medium heat, warm 1 tablespoon oil. Add the eggs and scramble until firm; transfer to a bowl. Add 2 tablespoons oil to the pan. Add the carrots and sauté until softened, about 2 minutes; transfer to the bowl with eggs. Add more oil to the pan, if needed, then add the tofu and sauté for 3–4 minutes, browning on all sides; transfer to the bowl with the eggs and carrots. Add more oil only if needed. Add the shrimp and sauté until just opaque and firm, 1–2 minutes; transfer to the bowl with eggs, carrots and tofu.

Raise the heat to medium-high. Add the daikon to the pan and sauté until it begins to soften, about 30 seconds; do not overcook. Add ¼ cup of the sauce and stir to coat well. Add the eggs, carrots, tofu, and shrimp and toss to coat with the sauce, adding more as desired.

Transfer the contents of the pan to a platter. Top with the bean sprouts and green onions and serve, passing the cilantro, peanuts, and lime wedges at the table.

SERVES 4–6

FOR THE SAUCE

½ teaspoon minced garlic

½ teaspoon minced serrano chile

2¼ oz palm sugar or light brown sugar

¼ cup tamarind paste

3 tablespoons Asian fish sauce

1 teaspoon fresh lime juice

1½–2 lb daikon radish

3 carrots

Canola oil, as needed

2 large eggs

5 oz extra-firm tofu, cubed

1 lb large shrimp, peeled and deveined

4 oz bean sprouts

2 green onions, thinly sliced

Fresh cilantro leaves, chopped roasted peanuts, and lime wedges for serving

Fish Tacos

WITH JICAMA SLAW

Crisp jicama spun into spiral noodles adds new visual appeal to a zesty Mexican-style slaw to top grilled fish tacos. The Spiralizer also shreds onions and cabbage in seconds. Serve extra slaw on the side.

6 tablespoons fresh lime juice

4 tablespoons olive oil

2 jalapeño chiles, seeded and finely chopped

½ teaspoon ground cumin

Kosher salt

1 small red onion, peeled and ends trimmed

1 small head red cabbage, top end trimmed

1 medium-sized jicama, peeled and ends trimmed

1 can (15-oz) black beans, drained and rinsed

1 ear fresh corn, kernels removed (about 1 cup kernels)

½ cup sliced green onions

¼ cup chopped fresh cilantro

1 lb tilapia or other white-fleshed fish fillets, cut in half lengthwise along their natural seam

1 teaspoon chili powder

8 corn tortillas, warmed

2 avocados, sliced

Lime wedges, for serving

In a small bowl, whisk together 5 tablespoons of the lime juice, 2 tablespoons of the olive oil, the jalapeños, cumin, and 1 teaspoon salt to make a vinaigrette. Set aside.

Cut a slit in one side of the red onion, stopping near the center. Spiralize the onion using the Straight Blade and transfer to a large bowl. Cut a slit in one side of the red cabbage, stopping near the center. Spiralize the cabbage using the Straight Blade and add it to the bowl with the onion. Cut a slit in one side of the jicama, stopping near the center. Spiralize the jicama using the Shredder Blade and transfer it to the bowl with the onion and cabbage.

Add the black beans, corn kernels, green onions, cilantro, and vinaigrette to the bowl with the vegetables and toss well. Set aside while you cook the fish.

Place the tilapia on a large plate and season lightly with salt. Sprinkle the chili powder evenly over the fish and drizzle with the remaining 1 tablespoon lime juice.

In a large nonstick frying pan over medium-high heat, warm the remaining 2 tablespoons olive oil. Working in 2 batches, sauté the fish until golden brown and opaque, about 2 minutes per side; keep warm.

To serve, divide the slaw among the tortillas. Divide the fish among the tortillas and top with avocado slices. Serve, passing the lime wedges at the table.

SERVES 4

Potato & Caramelized Onion Gratin

Who can resist a comforting potato gratin layered with Gruyère cheese? This dish updates the classic with thin spirals of potato, fresh herbs, and caramelized onions. The Spiralizer makes quick work of slicing the potatoes, so you can make this decadent side dish anytime.

2 yellow onions, peeled and ends trimmed

5 tablespoons olive oil, plus more for greasing

3 cloves garlic, minced

2 teaspoons chopped fresh thyme

4 russet potatoes (about 3½ lb total weight), ends trimmed

2 teaspoons kosher salt, plus more as needed

½ teaspoon freshly ground pepper

6 oz Gruyère cheese, shredded

Roughly chopped fresh flat-leaf parsley, for serving (optional)

Cut a slit in one side of each onion, stopping near the center. Spiralize the onions using the Straight Blade.

In a large sauté pan over medium-high heat, warm 3 tablespoons of the oil. Add the onion and sauté until browned and tender, about 15 minutes. Add the garlic and thyme and sauté until fragrant, about 1 minute. Transfer to a large bowl and let cool.

Preheat the oven to 400°F and lightly grease a 4-quart baking dish.

Spiralize the potatoes using the Shredder Blade, stopping to break or cut the strands every 3–4 rotations. Transfer the potatoes to the bowl with the onions and toss with remaining 2 tablespoons olive oil, the salt, pepper, and two-thirds of the Gruyère until well mixed. Transfer the mixture to the prepared dish and sprinkle the remaining Gruyère over the top. Cover the dish with foil and bake for 30 minutes. Remove the foil and continue to bake until the top is golden brown and a knife inserts easily into the center of the gratin, 20–30 minutes.

Let the gratin rest for 5 minutes before serving. Sprinkle with parsley, if desired, and serve.

SERVES 6–8

Kohlrabi, Fuji Apple & Kale Salad

Thin spirals of apple and kohlrabi join torn fresh kale in this crunchy fall salad, which is as satisfying as it is beautiful. Serve it alongside grilled chicken or salmon or add a little crumbled goat cheese or blue cheese for extra flavor and richness.

In a small bowl, whisk together the vinegar, brown sugar, mustard, and oil until the sugar is dissolved to make a vinaigrette. Season to taste with salt and pepper. Set aside.

Cut a slit in one side of the shallot, stopping near the center. Spiralize the shallot using the Straight Blade.

Spiralize the apples using the Shredder Blade, stopping to break or cut the strands every 2–3 rotations. Next, spiralize the kohlrabi in the same manner.

In a large bowl, toss together the shallots, apples, kohlrabi, and kale with vinaigrette to taste. Top with toasted pecans, and serve.

SERVES 6

3 tablespoons cider vinegar

1½ tablespoons firmly packed light brown sugar

1½ tablespoons whole-grain mustard

3 tablespoons olive oil

Kosher salt and freshly ground pepper

1 large shallot, peeled and ends trimmed

2 Fuji apples, ends trimmed

2 small kohlrabi, peeled, stalks and ends trimmed

1 bunch Tuscan kale, stemmed, leaves torn into bite-size pieces

1 bunch purple kale, stemmed, leaves torn into bite-size pieces

½ cup pecan halves, toasted and roughly chopped

TIP

Like with broccoli stalks, when working with kohlrabi, be sure to remove all of the fibrous peel from the vegetable before spiralizing.

Golden Beet Pasta

WITH BEET GREENS & GOAT CHEESE

Our entire test kitchen team fell in love with this dish. Sautéing the beet greens and folding them into the sauce creates a nice contrast of bitter against the sweet flavors of the pasta and vinaigrette.

Preheat the oven to 400°F.

Twist the stems off the beets. Separate the leaves from the stems and discard the stems. Soak the leaves in a bowl of cold water to remove the dirt, then rinse and dry in a salad spinner.

In a small bowl, whisk together the honey and vinegar. Stir in the shallot. While whisking, slowly pour in 4 tablespoons of the oil. Season with a generous pinch of salt and a few grinds of pepper to make a vinaigrette. Set aside.

Cut the beet greens into ½-inch slivers. In a nonstick frying pan over medium-high heat, warm 1 tablespoon of the oil. Add the beet greens along with a pinch of salt and sauté until wilted, about 2 minutes. Transfer the greens to a bowl and let cool.

Trim any remaining stems from the beets, then peel them. Spiralize the beets using the Shredder Blade, stopping to break or cut the strands every 3–4 turns. Transfer the beets to a large bowl. Toss the beets with the remaining 1 tablespoon oil and a pinch of salt. Divide the beets between 2 rimmed baking sheets and roast until the edges are barely brown, 8–10 minutes. Halfway through roasting, move the bottom baking sheet to the top rack and vice versa. When finished, the beets should still have a little bite to them.

Place the roasted beets in a large bowl. Add two-thirds of the vinaigrette, the beet greens, goat cheese, and walnuts. Toss to coat, adding more vinaigrette if needed, along with additional salt and pepper, and serve.

**SERVES 4 AS MAIN COURSE OR
6 AS A FIRST COURSE OR SIDE DISH**

2 lb golden beets with greens (4–6 beets)

2 tablespoons honey

2 tablespoons Champagne vinegar

½ shallot, minced (about 1 tablespoon)

6 tablespoons olive oil

Kosher salt and freshly ground pepper

4 oz goat cheese, crumbled

½ cup chopped walnuts, toasted

TIP

Spiralizing golden beets creates a beautiful texture that stands up to hearty sauces and flavors while bringing out the best in the beets. Peel the beets well so they maintain their vibrant color when roasted. The skin tends to look a little gray.

Butternut Squash Mac & Cheese

Macaroni and cheese is a comfort-food favorite. Substitute spiralized butternut squash to add a novel new flavor and beautiful appearance while adding additional nutrients to the dish.

2–3 butternut squashes, each 2½–3 lb, peeled

2 tablespoons olive oil

4 tablespoons unsalted butter

¼ cup all-purpose flour

2 cups milk

1 cup half-and-half

¼ teaspoon freshly grated nutmeg

Kosher salt and freshly ground pepper

1½ cups shredded Gruyère cheese

1½ cups shredded white Cheddar cheese

¼ cup grated Parmesan cheese

¼ cup panko bread crumbs

TIP

Instead of cooking the squash noodles in a frying pan, try roasting them on a sheet pan in a 400°F oven for 5–7 minutes. This will free up your hands to make the sauce.

Preheat an oven to 375°F.

Using a large knife, cut the butternut squashes crosswise, separating the dense, straight sections of the squash from the round parts that contain the seeds. Reserve the parts with the seeds for another use. Using the straight sections, spiralize the squash using the Chipper Blade.

In a large sauté pan over medium heat, warm the olive oil. Add the spiralized squash and sauté until soft, 7–10 minutes. Set aside.

In a saucepan over medium-high heat, melt the butter. Add the flour and cook, stirring well with a wooden spoon, until no visible flour remains, 1–3 minutes. Whisk in the milk, half-and-half, nutmeg, and a generous pinch of salt and bring to a boil. Simmer, whisking frequently to smooth out any lumps, until the sauce is thick and coats the back of a spoon, 4–5 minutes. Remove from the heat and add a pinch of pepper and 1 cup each of the Gruyère and Cheddar cheeses. Stir until smooth.

Pour the cheese sauce into the pan with the butternut squash noodles and stir well. Transfer to a 2¾-quart Dutch oven, or similar-sized pan. Top with the remaining Gruyère and Cheddar cheeses, the Parmesan, and panko. Bake until the top is lightly browned and the sauce is bubbly, 25–30 minutes. Let stand for 5 minutes before serving.

SERVES 4–6

Tri-Color Coleslaw
WITH BUTTERMILK DRESSING

Spiralizing the vegetables for this tangy slaw makes its assembly fast and easy. Try this with pulled pork or chicken, or as a side dish. For a lighter option, use Greek yogurt instead of buttermilk and mayonnaise.

Spiralize both heads of cabbage and the onion using the Straight Blade. (If you prefer smaller vegetable pieces, coarsely chop the cabbage and onions after spiralizing). Place the vegetables in a large bowl.

Spiralize the carrots using the Shredder Blade. Add them to the bowl with the cabbage and onions.

To make the dressing, in a bowl, combine the buttermilk, mayonnaise, agave nectar, vinegar, and 1 teaspoon salt and whisk until smooth. Taste, adding more salt and a few grinds of pepper as desired.

Pour half of the dressing over the cabbage mixture and toss to coat. Add more dressing as desired. Adjust the seasonings and serve, or cover and refrigerate for up to 1 day before serving.

SERVES 8

1 small head green cabbage (about 1 lb), top ends trimmed and outer leaves removed

1 small head purple cabbage (about 1 lb), top end trimmed and outer leaves removed

1 red onion, peeled and ends trimmed

2 carrots, peeled and ends trimmed

¾ cup buttermilk

¾ cup mayonnaise

¼ cup light agave nectar

¼ cup cider vinegar

Kosher salt and freshly ground pepper

TIP

If you like, stir ½ cup finely chopped mixed fresh herbs, such as flat-leaf parsley, dill, and basil, into the finished slaw.

Beet, Fennel & Carrot Salad

Colorful and nutritious, this simple salad will reignite your love affair with beets. For a delicious lunch on the go, pour the vinaigrette in the bottom of a large Mason jar. Layer the vegetables in the jar, then put the parsley on top, and seal. When you're ready to eat, shake well and enjoy.

3 tablespoons fresh lemon juice

2 tablespoons extra-virgin olive oil, plus more for drizzling

Kosher salt and freshly ground pepper

1 small bulb fennel, stalks removed, fronds reserved and chopped

2 large carrots, peeled and ends trimmed

1 medium-sized golden beet, peeled and ends trimmed

1 medium-sized red beet, peeled and ends trimmed

½ cup packed fresh flat-leaf parsley leaves

In a small bowl, whisk together the lemon juice, oil, 1 teaspoon salt, and ¼ teaspoon pepper to make a vinaigrette. Set aside.

Cut a slit in one side of the fennel, stopping near the center. Spiralize the fennel using the Shredder Blade (or Angel Hair Blade, if your model has one) and place in a large bowl.

Using the same blade, spiralize the carrots, golden beet, and red beet, stopping to break or cut the strands every 3–4 rotations. Add the carrots and beets to the bowl with the fennel.

Add the parsley and reserved fennel fronds to the bowl and toss to mix. Drizzle with the vinaigrette to taste, toss until well coated, and serve.

SERVES 4–6

TIP

Though it's an optional step, to minimize the bleeding effect of the red beets, you can rinse, then soak the spiralized beets in a bowl of cold water for 5–10 minutes, replacing the water with a fresh supply as it becomes tinged.

Zucchini Salad

WITH MINT-ALMOND PESTO

Here, zucchini spirals are coated with a bright mint pesto. The dish is so rich and full of flavor, it's hard to believe it's vegan! Choose your favorite combination of any or all of the herbs to customize the recipe.

½ cup firmly packed fresh mint leaves

¼ cup firmly packed fresh flat-leaf parsley leaves

¼ cup firmly packed fresh basil leaves

⅓ cup slivered almonds, toasted

2 cloves garlic, chopped

⅛ teaspoon red pepper flakes

Kosher salt

⅓ cup olive oil, plus more as needed

3 medium zucchini, ends trimmed

Finely grated zest of 1 lemon

To make the pesto, in a mini food processor, combine the mint, parsley, basil, toasted almonds, garlic, pepper flakes, and ½ teaspoon salt. Pulse until the ingredients are finely chopped. Add ⅓ cup of the oil and pulse until a coarse purée forms. Taste, adding more oil or salt as desired. Set aside.

Spiralize the zucchini using the Shredder Blade, stopping to break or cut the strands every 3–4 rotations. Place the zucchini in a serving bowl. Add the pesto and toss to coat, adding additional oil if needed to adjust the consistency. Sprinkle the lemon zest over the zucchini and toss again. Taste, adding additional salt if necessary, and serve.

SERVES 4

TIP

Zucchini tends to leach a lot of water. To minimize that, sprinkle spiralized zucchini with a generous pinch of salt, then allow them to drain in a colander for 30 minutes before tossing with the pesto.

Zucchini Noodles
WITH POACHED EGGS, SMOKED SALMON & CRÈME FRAÎCHE

Poached eggs, smoked salmon, and crème fraîche are a classic combination for brunch. The spiralized zucchini noodles elevate the dish by adding freshness and crunch.

Spiralize the zucchini using the Shredder Blade. Place the zucchini in a large colander, sprinkle with a pinch of salt, and toss to coat. Let the zucchini stand for about 30 minutes, or until some moisture is released.

In a mini food processor, combine the crème fraîche, lemon juice, garlic, dill, and ½ teaspoon salt. Pulse to mix and set aside.

Cut a slit in the side of each shallot, stopping just before the center. Spiralize the shallots using the Straight Blade. Add the shallots to a bowl along with the zucchini and crème fraîche mixture. Toss well.

To poach the eggs, fill a large saucepan with 2–3 inches of water and add the vinegar. Place over medium heat and bring to a gentle simmer. Break the eggs, one at a time, into a small bowl. Hold the bowl so it is just touching the simmering water and slide the egg into the water. Repeat with the remaining eggs, spacing them about 1 inch apart. Keeping the water at a gentle simmer, cook the eggs until the whites are set and the yolks are glazed over but still soft, 3–4 minutes.

To serve, divide the zucchini mixture among 4 plates and top with the salmon, dividing evenly. Top each portion with a poached egg, using a slotted spoon to remove it from the poaching water, and serve.

MAKES 4 SERVINGS

3–4 medium zucchini, ends trimmed

Kosher salt

¾ cup crème fraîche

2 tablespoons fresh lemon juice

1 clove garlic, minced

2 teaspoons chopped fresh dill

2 shallots

1 tablespoon white vinegar

4 large eggs

4 oz thinly sliced smoked salmon

Tortilla Española

WITH SMOKY ONIONS & ROASTED RED PEPPERS

We've added smoked paprika–spiked onions, roasted peppers, and nutty manchego cheese to the classic Spanish egg-and-potato dish.

Preheat the oven to 375°F. In a large bowl, whisk together the eggs, salt, pepper, chopped parsley, and manchego until blended. Set aside.

Cut a slit in one side of the onion, stopping near the center. Spiralize the onion using the Straight Blade.

In a 10-inch nonstick frying pan over medium-high heat, warm 2 tablespoons of the oil. Add the onion and sauté until browned and tender, about 10 minutes. Season lightly with salt. Add the smoked paprika and sauté until fragrant, about 1 minute. Transfer to a small bowl to cool.

Cut a slit in one side of each potato, stopping near the center. Spiralize the potatoes using the Straight Blade,

Return the pan to medium-high heat and warm the remaining 1 tablespoon oil. Add the potatoes and sauté until lightly browned and the centers are translucent, 8–10 minutes. Season lightly with salt. Sprinkle the onions and red pepper over the top. Reduce the heat to medium and pour in the egg mixture. Cook, without stirring, until the eggs begin to set around the edges, 1–2 minutes; occasionally run a silicone spatula around the edges to release the eggs from the pan sides. Transfer the pan to the oven. Bake until the edges are golden and the center is set, about 15 minutes. Let stand for 5 minutes.

Cut a slit in one side of the shallot, stopping near the center. Spiralize the shallot using the Straight Blade. In a bowl, toss the shallot slices with the parsley leaves, lemon juice, and extra-virgin olive oil. Season with salt.

Transfer the tortilla to a cutting board and slice it into 6 wedges. Transfer the wedges to individual plates. Top each wedge with some of the shallot-parsley salad, and serve.

SERVES 6

8 large eggs

½ teaspoon kosher salt, plus more as needed

¼ teaspoon freshly ground pepper

2 tablespoons roughly chopped fresh flat-leaf parsley, plus 1 cup packed fresh flat-leaf parsley leaves

4 oz manchego cheese, shredded

1 yellow onion, peeled and ends trimmed

3 tablespoons olive oil

1 teaspoon smoked Spanish paprika

1 lb Yukon gold potatoes, ends trimmed

1 red bell pepper, roasted, peeled, seeded and cut into ¼-inch slices

1 large shallot, peeled and ends trimmed

1 tablespoon fresh lemon juice

1 tablespoon extra-virgin olive oil

Poached Eggs in Potato Nests

Fine spirals of potatoes, fried into small nests, hold spinach, poached eggs, and a Dijon sauce for a conversation-starting brunch dish.

1 large russet potato, about 1 lb total weight, ends trimmed

Kosher salt and freshly ground black pepper

1 teaspoon sweet paprika

¼ teaspoon garlic powder

¼ teaspoon onion powder

Pinch of ground cayenne pepper

Canola oil for frying

FOR THE DIJON SAUCE

½ cup mayonnaise

2 tablespoons Dijon mustard

1 tablespoon lemon juice

2 tablespoons water

2–3 dashes hot-pepper sauce

1 tablespoon olive oil

1 lb baby spinach

4 large eggs, poached (see page 39 for method)

Spiralize the potato using the Shredder Blade (or Angel Hair blade, if your model has one) stopping to break or cut the strands every 2–3 rotations. Place the strands in a bowl and rinse with cold water until the water runs clear. Cover with fresh water and let stand for 20 minutes.

In a small bowl, mix together 2 teaspoons salt, ⅛ teaspoon black pepper, the paprika, garlic powder, onion powder, and cayenne. Set aside.

Into a high-sided saucepan, pour in 1 inch of canola oil. Place the pan over medium-high heat and warm the oil until it reaches 350°F on a deep-frying thermometer. Line a rimmed baking sheet with paper towels. When you are ready to fry, drain the potatoes well and pat thoroughly dry. Roughly divide the potato strands into 4 portions. Drop one-half of a portion into the hot oil, allowing any bubbles to dissipate before adding the rest of the portion. Using a skimmer, push the edges of the resulting potato nest toward the center and fry until golden brown, about 2 minutes. Carefully flip the nest and continue frying until the other side is golden, 2–3 more minutes. Carefully transfer the nest to the lined baking sheet and sprinkle with some of the spice mixture. Repeat with the remaining potato portions, adjusting the heat to maintain the oil temperature to between 350° and 375°F.

To make the Dijon sauce, in a small bowl, whisk together the sauce ingredients. In a large sauté pan over medium-high heat, warm the olive oil. Add half of the spinach and sauté, until the leaves are beginning to wilt. Add the remaining spinach and continue cooking until wilted, about 2 minutes. Season with salt and pepper to taste. Set aside.

To serve, divide the potato nests among plates. Divide the spinach among the nests and top each with a poached egg. Drizzle with the sauce, and serve.

SERVES 4

Sweet Potato Dutch Baby

A Dutch baby is a cross between a pancake and a crepe, but it's easier to prepare than both since it's baked in the oven. Adding spiralized sweet potato is a great way to get picky eaters to eat their vegetables.

3 large eggs

⅔ cup whole milk

⅔ cup all-purpose flour

¼ cup sugar

½ teaspoon vanilla extract

½ teaspoon ground cinnamon

¼ teaspoon freshly grated nutmeg

Kosher salt

1 medium orange-fleshed sweet potato, peeled and ends trimmed

4 tablespoons unsalted butter, cut into pieces

Maple syrup, for serving

Butter, for serving

Preheat the oven to 450°F. Place a 9- or 10-inch cast-iron frying pan in the oven while the oven preheats.

Put the eggs in a blender and blend on high speed until pale and frothy, about 30 seconds. Add the milk, flour, sugar, vanilla, cinnamon, nutmeg, and a pinch of salt and blend until smooth, about 1 minute. The batter will be thin.

Spiralize the sweet potatoes using the Shredder Blade.

Carefully remove the frying pan from the oven. Add the butter, swirling to coat the pan with the butter as it melts. When the butter is melted, pour the batter into the pan. Quickly scatter the spiralized sweet potatoes onto the batter. Immediately return the pan to the oven. Bake until the pancake is puffed and golden-brown and the edges are crisp, 15–20 minutes.

Cut the pancake into wedges and serve with the maple syrup and butter.

SERVES 4–6

Individual Pear Crisps

Here, sweet pears are thinly sliced, tossed with spices, and then baked with an easy, but tempting topping. Serve these charming desserts with vanilla ice cream, caramel sauce, or both.

Preheat the oven to 350°F. Lightly butter six 1-cup ramekins or ceramic baking dishes and arrange them on a rimmed baking sheet.

To make the topping, in the bowl of a stand mixer fitted with the paddle attachment, combine the flour, sugars, salt, granola, diced butter, cinnamon, and nutmeg. Mix on low speed until the mixture is crumbly and the butter is the size of peas. Set aside.

To make the filling, cut a slit into one side of each pear, stopping near the core. Spiralize the pears using the Straight Blade. In a large bowl, combine the pear slices, cornstarch, lemon juice, sugar, cinnamon, and nutmeg. Mix gently but well, ensuring that all of the pear slices are coated with the sugar mixture.

Fill each of the prepared ramekins three-fourths full with pear slices. Top each portion with 2–3 tablespoons of the topping. Bake until the crisps are bubbly and the topping is golden brown, 20–25 minutes. Let cool slightly before serving.

SERVES 6

FOR THE TOPPING

6 tablespoons cold unsalted butter, diced, plus butter for greasing

½ cup all-purpose flour

¼ cup sugar

¼ cup firmly packed brown sugar

¼ teaspoon kosher salt

½ cup prepared granola (without dried fruit)

½ teaspoon ground cinnamon

¼ teaspoon freshly grated nutmeg

FOR THE FILLING

3 large firm pears, peeled and ends trimmed

1 tablespoon cornstarch

2 tablespoons fresh lemon juice

3 tablespoons sugar

1 teaspoon ground cinnamon

¼ teaspoon freshly grated nutmeg

Vanilla-Spiced Apple & Pear Chips

Fruit chips are a simple and creative way to snack on fruit. The apples get crisp, while the pears retain a pleasing chewy quality. These went quickly when we made them, so if you have the luxury of 2 ovens or extra time, double the recipe to allow for leftovers.

Preheat the oven to 225°F. Line 2 rimmed baking sheets with silicone baking mats or parchment paper.

In a small bowl, mix together the sugar, cinnamon, and ground vanilla.

Cut the tops and bottoms off of the apple and pear to create flat surfaces. Cut a slit in one side of the apple and the pear, stopping near the core. Spiralize the fruits using the Straight Blade. Arrange the fruit slices in a single layer on the prepared baking sheets. Sprinkle the fruit slices with the sugar-spice mixture. Bake for 1 hour.

Remove the baking sheets from the oven. Using your fingers or a small offset spatula, lift up the fruit slices from the pan (so they don't stick), and place them back on the pan in a single layer. Continue to bake the chips until dry and crisp, about 1 hour more.

Transfer the chips from the baking sheet to a cooling rack and let them stand for a few minutes to crisp up further. Serve, or cool completely and store in an airtight container for up to 2 days.

SERVES 2

1 tablespoon sugar

½ teaspoon ground cinnamon

¼ teaspoon ground vanilla bean or freshly grated nutmeg

1 Granny Smith apple

1 Bartlett pear

TIP

There is no need to peel the apples or pears. They are a beautiful part of the finished recipe. Ground vanilla bean can be found at Williams-Sonoma and specialty grocery stores.

Spiced Apple Cake

Spiralized apples are folded into this spiced cake as well as baked on top for an extra apple kick and beautiful presentation. This cake is versatile; it can be topped with ice cream or confectioners' sugar for a delicious dessert, or served for breakfast for a sweet start to the day.

1½ cups all-purpose flour

2 teaspoons baking powder

¼ teaspoon kosher salt

1½ teaspoons ground cinnamon

¼ teaspoon freshly grated nutmeg

3 firm apples, such as Gala or Granny Smith, peeled

½ cup unsalted butter, softened

½ cup, plus 2 tablespoons granulated sugar

½ cup firmly packed light brown sugar

2 large eggs

1 teaspoon pure vanilla extract

Preheat oven to 350°F. Spray a 9-inch springform pan with nonstick cooking spray.

In a bowl, whisk together the flour, baking powder, salt, ¾ teaspoon of the cinnamon, and the nutmeg.

Spiralize 1 apple using the Shredder Blade and then roughly chop; set aside. Spiralize the remaining 2 apples using the same blade, but don't chop; set aside separately.

In the bowl of a stand mixer fitted with the paddle attachment, beat the butter, ½ cup of the granulated sugar, and the brown sugar until the mixture is pale and fluffy, 2–3 minutes. Add the eggs 1 at a time, beating well after each addition. Beat in the vanilla extract. Turn the mixer on low speed, then add the flour mixture and mix until just combined; do not overmix. Fold in the chopped apple. Pour the batter into the prepared pan, spreading it evenly. In a bowl, toss the remaining spiralized apples with the remaining 2 tablespoons sugar and the remaining ¾ teaspoon cinnamon, then scatter over the top of the batter.

Bake until cake is golden brown and a toothpick inserted in the center comes out clean, 40–45 minutes. Let the cake cool in the pan for 10 minutes, then remove side of pan.

Cut the cake into wedges and serve warm or at room temperature.

SERVES 8–10

Spiralized Carrot Cake

The Spiralizer saves time when grating the carrots for this simple-to-put-together cake. Topped with a classic cream cheese frosting, it's perfect for any occasion.

FOR THE CAKE

Butter, for greasing

2 cups all-purpose flour, plus more for the pan

1¼ lb carrots, peeled, ends trimmed

2 teaspoons baking soda

2 teaspoons baking powder

2 teaspoons ground cinnamon

½ teaspoon ground allspice

½ teaspoon kosher salt

4 large eggs

¾ cup canola oil

¾ cup granulated sugar

1 cup firmly packed light brown sugar

½ cup buttermilk

FOR THE FROSTING

1 lb cream cheese, softened

1 cup unsalted butter, softened

4 cups confectioners' sugar

2 teaspoons vanilla extract

Position a rack in the center of the oven and preheat to 350°F. Butter and flour two 9-inch round cake pans.

Spiralize the carrots using the Shredder Blade and roughly chop; you should have about 3 cups. In a bowl, sift together the flour, baking soda, baking powder, cinnamon, allspice, and salt. In a large bowl, whisk together the eggs, oil, granulated sugar, brown sugar, and buttermilk. Stir the flour mixture into the egg mixture just until combined. Fold in the spiralized carrots.

Divide the batter evenly between the prepared pans. Bake the cakes until a toothpick inserted into the center comes out clean, about 40 minutes. Transfer the cakes to racks and let cool in the pans for 15 minutes. Invert the cakes onto the racks and cool completely.

To make the frosting, in a large bowl, combine the cream cheese and butter. Using an electric mixer on medium-high speed, beat until smooth. Reduce the speed to low, add the confectioners' sugar, and beat until smooth. Beat in the vanilla until well blended.

To assemble, place 1 cake layer on a plate. Spread 1½ cups of the frosting over the top. Place the second cake layer on top. Spread the remaining frosting over the top and sides of the cake. Serve right away, or refrigerate for up to 2 days.

SERVES 10–12

Index

A

Almond-mint pesto, with zucchini salad, 38
Angel hair blade, about, 8
Apple & pear chips, vanilla-spiced, 47
Apple
    cake, spiced, 48
    Fuji apple, kohlrabi, and kale salad, 29

B

Beef and broccoli, garlicky, with
    broccoli noodles, 17
Beet greens, with golden beet pasta and
    goat cheese, 31
Beet pasta, golden, with beet greens
    and goat cheese, 31
Beet, fennel, and carrot salad, 36
Beets, working with, 31, 36
Blades for the spiralizer, 8
Breakfast and brunch
    poached eggs in potato nests, 42
    sweet potato Dutch baby, 44
    tortilla española, 41
    zucchini noodles with poached eggs,
        smoked salmon, and crème fraîche, 39
Broccoli
    and beef, garlicky, with
        broccoli noodles, 17
    noodles, with garlicky beef
        and broccoli, 17
    stalks, spiralizing, 17
Buttermilk dressing, with
    tri-color coleslaw, 35
Butternut squash mac & cheese, 32

C

Cabbage, in tri-color coleslaw with
    buttermilk dressing, 35
Cake
    spiced apple, 48
    spiralized carrot, 50
Carrot
    carrot cake, spiralized, 50

carrot, beet, and fennel salad, 36
carrot salad, with Moroccan-spiced
    roasted chicken, 21
Carrots, in tri-color coleslaw with
    buttermilk dressing, 35
Cheese
    butternut squash mac & cheese, 32
    golden beet pasta with beet greens and
        goat cheese, 31
    Greek-style chicken pitas with cucumber
        salad and herbed yogurt, 22
    potato and caramelized onion gratin, 28
    tortilla española with smoky onions and
        roasted red peppers, 41
    zucchini spaghetti with
        turkey meatballs, 18
Chicken
    chicken pitas, Greek-style, with cucumber
        salad and herbed yogurt, 22
    Moroccan-spiced roasted chicken with
        carrot salad, 21
Chipper blade, about, 8
Coleslaw, tri-color, with
    buttermilk dressing, 35
Cream cheese, in spiralized carrot cake, 50
Cucumber salad, with Greek-style chicken
    pitas and herbed yogurt, 22

D

Desserts
    individual pear crisps, 45
    spiced apple cake, 48
    spiralized carrot cake, 50
Dutch baby, sweet potato, 44

E–F

Eggs
    poached, in potato nests, 42
    spiced apple cake, 48
    spiralized carrot cake, 50
    sweet potato Dutch baby, 44

tortilla española with smoky onions and
    roasted red peppers, 41
zucchini noodles with poached eggs,
    smoked salmon, and crème fraîche, 39
Fennel, beet & carrot salad, 36

G

Garlicky beef and broccoli with
    broccoli noodles, 17
Golden beet pasta with beet greens and
    goat cheese, 31
Greek-style chicken pitas with cucumber
    salad and herbed yogurt, 22

I

Individual pear crisps, 45

K

Kale, kohlrabi, and fuji apple salad, 29
Kohlrabi, Fuji apple, and kale salad, 29
Kohlrabi, working with, 29

M

Mac & cheese, butternut squash, 32
Main dishes
    butternut squash mac & cheese, 32
    garlicky beef and broccoli with
        broccoli noodles, 17
    golden beet pasta with beet greens
        and goat cheese, 31
    Greek-style chicken pitas with cucumber
        salad and herbed yogurt, 22
    Moroccan-spiced roasted chicken with
        carrot salad, 21
    zucchini spaghetti with turkey
        meatballs, 18
Mint-almond pesto, with zucchini salad, 38
Moroccan-spiced roasted chicken with
    carrot salad, 21

N

Nuts
    golden beet pasta with beet greens and
        goat cheese, 31

Kohlrabi, Fuji apple, and kale salad, 29
zucchini salad with mint-almond pesto, 38

O

Onion
    caramelized onion and potato gratin, 28
    Greek-style chicken pitas with cucumber
        salad and herbed yogurt, 22
    tri-color coleslaw with
        buttermilk dressing, 35
    Moroccan-spiced roasted chicken with
        carrot salad, 21
    Potato and caramelized onion gratin, 28
Onions, smoky, and roasted red peppers
    with tortilla española, 41

P

Pear and apple chips, vanilla-spiced, 47
Pear crisps, individual, 45
Pesto, mint-almond, with zucchini salad, 38
Poached eggs
    poached eggs in potato nests, 42
    poached eggs with smoked salmon, and
        crème fraîche, with zucchini noodles, 39
Potato and caramelized onion gratin, 28
Potato nests, poached eggs in, 42
Potatoes, in tortilla española with smoky
    onions and roasted red peppers, 41

R

Red peppers, roasted, and smoky onions
    with tortilla española, 41
Rice noodles, in garlicky beef and
    broccoli with broccoli noodles, 17
Roasted chicken, Moroccan-spiced, with
    carrot salad, 21
Roasted red peppers and smoky onions
    with tortilla española, 41

S

Salads
    beet, fennel & carrot salad, 36
    carrot, beet & fennel, 36
    kohlrabi, Fuji apple, and kale salad, 29

tri-color coleslaw with
buttermilk dressing, 35
zucchini salad with almond-mint pesto, 38
Sandwiches, Greek-style chicken pitas
with cucumber salad and herbed
yogurt, 22
Shredder blade, about, 8
Side dishes
beet, fennel & carrot salad, 36
butternut squash mac & cheese, 32
golden beet pasta with beet greens
and goat cheese, 31
kohlrabi, Fuji apple, and kale salad, 29
potato & caramelized onion gratin, 28
tri-color coleslaw with buttermilk
dressing, 35
zucchini salad with mint-almond pesto, 38
Skirt steak, in garlicky beef and broccoli
with broccoli noodles, 17
Smoked salmon, with zucchini noodles,
poached eggs, and crème fraîche, 39
Snacks, vanilla-spiced apple
& pear chips, 47
Spaghetti, zucchini, with turkey meatballs, 18
Spiced apple cake, 48
Spinach, in poached eggs in potato nests, 42
Spiralized carrot cake, 50
Spiralizer
blades, 8
parts, 11
how to use, 10
ways to use, 7
Spiralizing
about, 7
avoiding overcooking, 13
broccoli stalks, 17
centering the food on the machine, 13
choosing the right vegetable, 13
customizing noodle size, 13
cutting or breaking noodles, 13
foods to use, 8
primer, 10
reducing excess moisture, 13
saving time when slicing, 13
slicing round vegetables, 13

tips and tricks, 13
working with cabbage, 14
working with carrots, 14
working with fruit, 14
making curly fries, 14
Squash, butternut, mac & cheese, 32
Straight blade, about, 8
Sweet potato Dutch baby, 44

T
Tomatoes
Greek-style chicken pitas with cucumber
salad and herbed yogurt, 22
zucchini spaghetti with turkey
meatballs, 18
Tortilla española with smoky onions and
roasted red peppers, 41
Tri-color coleslaw with
buttermilk dressing, 35
Turkey meatballs, with
zucchini spaghetti, 18

V–W
Vanilla-spiced apple & pear chips, 47
Welcome to spiralizing, 7

Y–Z
Yogurt, in Greek-style chicken pitas
with cucumber salad and herbed
yogurt sauce, 22
Zucchini
tips for, 18
working with, 38
Zucchini noodles with poached
eggs, smoked salmon, and
crème fraîche, 39
Zucchini salad with mint-almond
pesto, 38
Zucchini spaghetti with
turkey meatballs, 18

THE SPIRALIZER COOKBOOK

Conceived and produced by Weldon Owen, Inc.
In collaboration with Williams-Sonoma, Inc.
3250 Van Ness Avenue, San Francisco, CA 94109

A WELDON OWEN PRODUCTION

1045 Sansome Street, Suite 100
San Francisco, CA 94111
www.weldonowen.com

WELDON OWEN, INC.

VP, Publisher Roger Shaw
VP, Sales and Marketing Amy Kaneko
Director of Finance Philip Paulick

Associate Publisher Jennifer Newens
Associate Editor Emma Rudolph

Creative Director Kelly Booth
Art Directors Debbie Berne & Marisa Kwek
Senior Production Designer Rachel Lopez Metzger

Production Director Chris Hemesath
Associate Production Director Michelle Duggan

Photographer Maren Caruso
Food Stylist Kim Kissling

Printed and bound by Worzalla, USA

First printed in 2014
10 9 8 7 6 5 4 3 2 1

Library of Congress Cataloging-in-Publication
data is available.

ISBN13: 978-1-61628-915-7
ISBN 10: 1-61628-915-5

Weldon Owen is a division of **BONNIER**

ACKNOWLEDGMENTS

Weldon Owen wishes to thank the following people for their
generous support in producing this book:
Emily Garland and Taylor Louie